Peace and War in today's world

by
Craig M. White

All booklets are published thanks to the generous support of the members of the Catholic Truth Society

CATHOLIC TRUTH SOCIETY
PUBLISHERS TO THE HOLY SEE

Contents

Peace: the Ultimate Reality

The Bible begins with a picture of a garden where peace is so deep that human beings do not even need clothes. Harmony is so profound that there is not even the disrespect, not even the snickering, that nakedness might lead to. Then conflict enters the world, first between man and God, and then between man and woman. Conflict ripens into murder by Chapter 4, and into war by Chapter 14. But the Bible ends with a picture of a city full of trees with a river flowing through it, a city where the peace is so complete that the gates of the city are never shut, and "There shall no more be anything accursed" (Revelation 22:3). Peace, in each soul, between all created beings, and with God, is the original and ultimate reality.

We find ourselves, however, between the original and the ultimate peace, in a world of war, of conflict, of power exercised for domination and destruction, of suffering and early death. It is a world with a great deal of evil. That evil has, at the very least, a foothold in each one of us, so even when we think we are doing good, we must be wary of doing evil.

A Divine Gift, a Human Work

Like the kingdom of God, peace is both a gift of God and a human work. Because of this, the Church is meant to ask God continually for the gift of peace, and to work tirelessly to accomplish it. One of the marks of his followers, as Jesus noted in the Sermon on the Mount, is that they are peace-makers. In seeking and helping to make peace, we show ourselves to be the children of God because he is the ultimate source of peace.[1]

Peace Comes from Harmony built on Justice

"Peace is not just the absence of war. . . . Like a cathedral, peace must be constructed patiently and with unshakable faith," as Pope John Paul II once said. Rightly understood, the peace Catholics celebrate in this world is an orderly harmony. It is not the result of harsh control by violent human rulers, but is built on an understanding of the character of God and the dignity of the human beings he has created to live in "freedom, justice, truth, and love."[2] "Peace results from that harmony built into human society by its divine founder and actualised by men as they thirst after ever greater justice." Isaiah calls peace "the effect of righteousness" (Isaiah 32:17).[3]

May Peace-Makers Ever Make War?

While we should all work to build peace on the basis of justice, in this world there are competing powers using force, sometimes to do what is clearly evil. What can and should we do about that evil? Many Catholic saints were martyrs who made no attempt to fight back against those who tormented them, but oddly enough, we also have as an example St Louis, the warrior king. How can war, with all the suffering and death it causes, ever be right? What is the Catholic position on self-defense for a nation? Is one country right to help another country resist invasion or theft? Is one country justified in invading another country to depose a tyrant, seize a terrorist leader, or end some horrible state of affairs? Were the Crusades justified? What are the reasons for the Catholic Church's teachings about war and peace? Although we accept by faith that peace is the ultimate reality, the bulk of this booklet will be about war, in an attempt to answer some of the complex issues and questions it raises.

Jesus, the Early Church, and War

Was Jesus a Pacifist?

Most people begin with the question, "didn't Jesus say to turn the other cheek? Wasn't he a pacifist? Tolstoy and Gandhi seem to think so." Although it will be argued here that there is a limited place for force, in defense of self and others, we must agree that the willingness of our Lord and of many Christians throughout history to suffer violence without responding in kind expresses something fundamental about God and about our faith. At the heart of that faith is a self-giving love that does not count the cost, even if the cost is suffering violence, sometimes to the point of death. It is this kind of love that won so much of the world to the faith, and to the Catholic Church in particular.

The Church in fact teaches that the use of force is sometimes justified, for both individuals and for nations. For example, it is just for anyone to use force to defend himself against an actual attack, or to defend the helpless when they are being attacked. However, the use of force by an individual is only right under certain carefully defined conditions. The same is true for nations: the Church teaches that the use of force is justified under "strict conditions" requiring "rigorous" consideration, and it is clearly easy to misinterpret those conditions as allowing the use of force when they do not (or as allowing unlimited use of force). It should be stressed, however, that the fact that the Church teaches that war is sometimes justified does not mean that it approves of all the wars announced by Christian rulers.

The testimony of the early Church may at first glance appear to require non-violence for all, and at all times, in an apparent sharp change from the Old Testament. Jesus not only called peacemakers "sons of God," but commanded "turning the other cheek." He told his followers to carry swords at one point, but when Peter used one, Jesus told him to "Put your sword back into its place; for all who take the sword will perish by the sword" (Matthew 26:52, John 18:10). Jesus, of course, did not resist those who arrested, tortured, and killed him. Was this teaching and example absolute, or was it for himself and some of his followers only, or for some times and not others?

Some of our Lord's early followers seemed to think it absolute. St Martin of Tours, a soldier (and the patron saint of soldiers!), is said to have refused to take part in a battle in AD 336, declaring, "I am a soldier of Christ. I cannot fight." Other Christian leaders made statements, especially before Christianity became legal, that appear to rule out soldiering as a Christian occupation.[4] However, there was disagreement within the early Church on a number of topics, and certainly there is no definitive early statement ruling out war. Catholics are bound by the definitive teaching of the Church in matters of faith and morals, and there simply was no such teaching at the time. There are some good reasons to believe that the example and teaching of Jesus and the writings of the New Testament did not forbid Christians to use force in all circumstances.

The Nightmare of Persecution

Before getting to those reasons, consider the situation of the early church. For almost 300 years, Christians in the Roman Empire, where the faith was born and the vast majority lived, were in a precarious position. The State was seen as both a political and a religious community. The Emperor was considered to be divine, and every good, patriotic citizen, whatever other religion he might follow, could also be required at any time to offer a pinch of incense in worship to the Emperor via his statue. Not to do so was a kind of treason and heresy combined, total disloyalty to the State.

Jews were exempt from this rule (the Romans realising that they might have to exterminate them to enforce it). In the very early years, it appears that Roman officials often considered the Christian faith a branch of Judaism, which in one sense it is. However, after some decades, they decided that Christians were different enough not to deserve the exemption. That meant: sacrifice, or die. If you believed in many gods, or were a skeptical philosopher, you might reason that a pinch of incense to a false god was nothing to lose sleep over, but Christians took the First Commandment, "you shall have no other gods before me," very seriously: Caesar was not God, and only God could be worshipped. As a result, Christians, a large percentage of whom were slaves, the poor, and other social outcasts, were a convenient scapegoat for the government for about 250 years, and suffered greatly. Since the army helped enforce these persecutions, as well as torturing, crucifying, and otherwise viciously abusing enemies of the State, Christians naturally avoided being soldiers. Soldiers who converted to Christianity sometimes tried to leave the army.

The New Reality: Legal Christianity

When the Emperor Constantine legalised Christianity in the Edict of Milan in AD 313, Christians were delirious with joy. Since many people now, looking back from the present, bitterly criticise the changes in Christian practice after Constantine came to power, it is worth putting ourselves in the places of Christians at the time. Let us remember that every few decades since Nero began the custom in AD 64, Roman officials had started official pogroms (lasting years) against Christians, leading to the deadly choice again and again: renounce your faith, or be viciously tortured and die an agonising death. If you ran away, all your property was seized. The last two major episodes of persecution have been called "total war against the Catholic Church." When your religion is declared legal after two and a half centuries of such treatment, your joy is understandable! The story quickly spread that before the battle of Milvian Bridge in AD 312 Constantine had a vision or dream in which a cross appeared in the sky, and a voice declared, "in this sign you shall conquer." Constantine had his soldiers paint crosses (or the first two Greek letters of the word "Christ"—the stories differ on the details) on their shields before the battle. His decisive victory brought him to full power in the western half of the Empire.[5]

Soon, Christianity became the official religion of the whole Empire. The religion of the poor and persecuted became the religion of many of the rich and powerful as well. Many see this enormous change as leading immediately to the complete perversion of true Christianity, but this is an odd position. Judaism was not destroyed when the Israelites entered the Promised Land. Stoics did not think their philosophy was perverted because Emperor Marcus Aurelius adopted it. In science, a true theory is sometimes accepted by the great and powerful, which does not lead to its total perversion. It is true that hypocrisy became a far greater danger than before, but that is simply a danger whenever moral truth receives lip service from the powerful. And if Christianity is true, how could it not be true for rulers as well as the ruled? Islam has a different issue: its prophet became a military leader and a political ruler in his lifetime, and some Muslims are proud to point out that they have no division between "God and Caesar," because all is God's. In fact, because Christ made a place for Caesar as well as God ("Render therefore to Caesar the things that are Caesar's," Matthew 22:21), and died a shameful death, and because his followers were a persecuted minority for almost 300 years, Christianity naturally sees a difference between church and state, which have different functions (and should have different leaders). This vision of a difference between church and state led eventually (with some non-Christian help, after some admittedly awful Christian practices) to the Christian theory and practice of religious freedom for all.[6]

Just War Theory

Over time, and building on earlier ideas, thinkers in the Church developed criteria for the use of force by governments in a variety of situations. The criteria for using force in war make up what is known as just war theory. The theory has two main branches, one of which (known in Latin as *ius ad bellum*) is used to evaluate whether going to war is just in a given situation, and the other (*ius in bello*) to evaluate the rightness of actions once a nation has begun a war. As centuries went by, the theory was developed and used by non-Catholics and non-Christians as well, and is still widely used for moral guidance concerning war.

Biblical Roots

In Constantine's time, Christian emperors meant Christian generals and soldiers, and this naturally led to some new thinking about war. The Lord's words still stood: so could an army led by and including Christians exist? Some, as we have seen, would say that when Christianity was adopted by a warlike Roman emperor, it was corrupted from its pure non-violent beginnings into something new and bad. At the time, however, theologians like St Augustine found plenty of biblical reasons explaining why a limited use of force by government was right. Augustine pointed out that John the Baptist told repentant Roman soldiers who asked what they should do, "Rob no one by violence or by false accusation, and be content with your wages"[7], John did not tell them to give up soldiering. Theologians may have noticed that although converts were called to a completely new way of life, one of the first non-Jewish converts, the Roman officer Cornelius, hears nothing from St Peter about changing his job (Acts 10). They certainly pointed out St Paul's warning, "if you do wrong, be afraid, for he does not bear the sword in vain; he is the servant of God to execute his wrath on the wrongdoer" (Romans 13:4). Paul's warning grants the right of authorities to use force, but only, as in the Old Testament, to enforce what is right, not to indulge their personal whims or to gain wealth and power. Augustine began his comment on John the Baptist with the words, "if the Christian religion forbade war altogether,"[8] showing that from his perspective, there were strict conditions on the warfare allowed to Christians. Still, despite the horrible abuse of force at the founding of and in the early centuries of Christianity, Church teaching now announced clearly that force, strictly limited and properly directed, had its place as a response to evil, just as it did in the Old Testament, with its many warrior kings and heroes.

Sources in Reason and the Classical World

Theologians such as Augustine not only knew the Bible and holy church tradition, they were also educated men of their time. As such, they were shaped by the classical Greek and Roman culture, which, like all cultures, had some ideas about war and justice. Believing that God is Reason (Logos), not just Being and Will and Power, or even Love, as Pope Benedict has pointed out[9], Catholic theologians looked to thinkers like Aristotle and Cicero to see what they might have to say about war, as well as other subjects.

Some of Aristotle's ideas were never accepted by the Church. He stated, for example, that wars to acquire slaves and territory were "naturally just," if the people who were conquered were those who "ought to be governed" by others. On the other hand, Aristotle said more positively that although war had its uses, it was not noble in itself. He said any leader who made war for its own sake would be "a bloodthirsty monster," and claimed, "we make war in order that we may live at peace."[10]

Cicero placed more restrictions on war, and is perhaps the first person to provide a list of criteria that a war should meet in order to be just. His list either states or hints that to be just a war must be "duly announced and proclaimed," and must have a just cause and a proper motive, as well as "a prior demand for restitution." To the modern way of thinking, this last demand sounds strange, but in the ancient world, most conflicts could be settled by restitution or a large enough monetary payment to compensate the innocent for their losses, so the reasoning here is that such a demand must be made before a war may be started. Discussion, the method rational beings use to settle conflicts, must always be tried before war, he wrote. Cicero also insisted that after victory in a just war, mercy should be shown to those who had not been "bloodthirsty and barbarous" in their way of fighting. This implied that a nation with a just cause is not entitled by that just cause to fight any way it likes, but must also fight justly.[11]

Augustine did not write a systematic treatise on the subject of war and peace, but dropped hints on the subject in many places in his writings. He quoted Cicero, obviously agreed with him that some wars are just and some are not, and laid down a number of thoughts on what might make a war just or unjust. He recognised a legitimate use of force by those in authority, but insisted that among rational creatures such as human beings, rule by one over another is not "natural."[12] Such domination, though legitimate in this world, is a result of sin, and was not part of God's original plan. He laid down a very high standard for rulers, saying that a just ruler acted as the servant of those he ruled. Augustine described even just wars as "miseries" and "evils,"[13] writing that if anyone could think of them "without mental pain," that person "has lost human feeling."

When it is Right to Go to War

The Criteria

St Thomas Aquinas, writing many centuries later, was the first Christian thinker to address systematically the question of when a war is just or unjust, or to put it another way, when it is right to go to war. This is the *ius ad bellum*, from the Latin for (roughly) "right in going to war." Aquinas' short discussion of war[14] comes under the heading "whether war is always sinful," and addresses war under a list of things, "discord, contention, schism, war, strife, sedition, scandal" that are opposed to the virtue of peace. (It seems that he was not writing of defensive wars, as those would automatically be just, in the same way that self-defense is just for one person, unless the country being attacked has committed some grave injustice, and owes some kind of reparation to the attacking country and has refused to meet its obligations.)[15] Although the context is a discussion of sin, Aquinas appealed to the common sense of his readers as well as to the Bible and earlier theologians.

Aquinas denied that war is always sinful, but made it clear that it is sinful unless it meets conditions. He wrote that, "in order for a war to be just, three things are necessary." Those three things are sovereign authority, a just cause, and a right intention.

Sovereign Authority

The authority of the sovereign, or ruler, is necessary according to Aquinas because a private individual can and should seek the righting of wrongs through higher officials. In addition, the ruler is the one who is responsible for the common good, who is authorized to use force for that purpose if necessary, and who is authorized to call people together for a common task, which is necessary for war. The *Catholic Catechism* translates "the sovereign" into modern terms as "those who have responsibility for the common good."[16] We all have some responsibility for the common good, but in every society there are individuals with delegated powers to take certain decisions or actions for the common good: legislatures pass laws, courts hear cases and issue rulings, and so forth. There is always a group or an individual with the authority to declare or lead a war (although that authority may be split between different groups or individuals).

A Just Cause

In explaining a just cause, Aquinas wrote of a war that "avenges wrongs, when a nation or state has to be punished, for refusing to make amends for the wrongs inflicted by its subjects, or to restore what it has seized unjustly." The *Catechism* speaks of "lasting" and "grave" "damage inflicted by the aggressor on the nation or community of nations." It should be clear that expanding one's nation's territory, grabbing more resources, or rearranging the international scene to one's liking are not *just* causes.

Right Intention

Coming to right intention, we reach the heart of the matter. Not only an outwardly just cause is necessary, but an inward right motivation. Aquinas insists that those starting a just war must "intend the advancement of good, or the avoidance of evil." A just war will be waged for motives of "securing peace, of punishing evil-doers, and of uplifting the good," but never "for motives of aggrandisement or cruelty," nor out of "the cruel thirst for vengeance" or "the lust of power." In fact, the positive aspect of right intention is "the aim of peace." This should not be merely a pious *wish* to achieve peace. An intention in Aquinas' thought is something firmly connected to the choice of means. In other words, if we truly intend something, we will choose means to that end which are likely to achieve it. If you "intend" in this sense to motor across the Sahara, for example, you will ensure that you have a suitable vehicle, spare tires, knowledge of the terrain and the political situation in each country, money to buy fuel and spare fuel cans to carry it for the stretches where no fuel is available, maps, necessary visas, etc. Failure to choose such realistic means equals failure to meet the criterion of a right intention.[17]

Three More Criteria

More recently, three more criteria were added to Aquinas' classic three, namely proportionality of ends, last resort, and reasonable chance of success. These three criteria are in complete harmony with Aquinas' teaching on moral action, something easy to demonstrate.[18] Concerning proportionality of ends, the *Catechism* states that "the use of arms must not produce evils and disorders graver than the evil to be eliminated," and warns that "the power of modern means of destruction weighs very heavily in evaluating this condition." The *Catechism* explains "last resort" as meaning that "all other means of putting an end to [the grave injustice] must have been shown to be impractical or ineffective." Reasonable chance of success is self-explanatory: launching a war that has no hope of succeeding cannot be just, no matter how just the cause.

Note that all three of these last criteria, along with right intention, require a common definition of "success," or the aim for which the war is fought. This is never simply the defeat of enemy military forces, but includes "the aim of peace." If a tyrant is to be overthrown, success will involve replacing his government with a better one. A just war, in other words, depends not only on proper authority and a just cause, but also on a clear, realistic vision of what the warring country hopes to achieve in the country to be fought, and an intention to achieve it. It also depends on realistic planning that shows that a war can achieve the desired result, that the war will not cause greater evil than it plans to overcome, and that war can succeed in producing that desired result.

Strict Conditions, Rigorously Considered

Together, these six criteria are quite satisfying to most people, at least as an ideal. They allow war, but only when it is truly aimed at a good end. They assume that all societies have a right not to be attacked, unless they have committed some grave evil, and even then the only justification for war is to redress that evil and (an amazing requirement, when you think about it) to establish peace. Greatness and ambition create no right to take a square foot of territory or an ounce of mineral wealth. No religious, racial, or cultural superiority justifies war, in this view.

The six criteria constitute a high moral standard that has appealed to both religious and non-religious people for centuries. The *Catechism* rightly insists that these are "strict conditions" that "require rigorous consideration." In other words, if you read a few quick sentences or brief paragraphs proclaiming that a war is just, even if they quote from just war theory, you should be concerned that the argument is almost certainly inadequate, unless it is summarizing a case that is made elsewhere in far more detail. A just war case should include objective definitions that are applied to all sides and should answer objections fairly and in detail. As Catholic writer George Weigel points out, for Catholics "stuff counts."[19] The six criteria must be applied to the thick, detailed reality of the world. The justice of the cause should be beyond reasonable doubt, and the planning for that "success" that is "the aim of peace" should be as thorough as time permits. As the *Catechism* notes, "because of the evils and injustices that all war brings with it, we must do everything reasonably possible to avoid it," including and especially prayer.

The Moral Dangers of Even a Just War

There is a long Catholic lay tradition of celebrating the warriors who take part in a just war. As the Catholic writer Hilaire Belloc wrote, "I…told him that armies fighting in a just cause were the happiest places for living, and that a good battle for justice was the beginning of all great songs."[20]

Celebrating Victory

We can read Chesterton's poem "Lepanto," and meditate on the 10,000 or so mostly Christian galley slaves freed by the Christian forces at the end of the battle. A Turkish victory at Lepanto would have opened many Christian countries to Islamic conquest, with all the discrimination against Christianity and the encouragement to convert to Islam that entailed. At the Vatican, paintings on the walls of at least one hallway are dedicated to the victory there. And C.S. Lewis writes, "The idea of the knight—the Christian in arms for the defence of a good cause—is one of the great Christian ideas." He goes on to complain about "this sort of semi-pacifism" that "robs lots of magnificent young Christians in the Services of something…which is the natural accompaniment of courage—a kind of gaiety and wholeheartedness."[21]

Mental Pain

Yet, as noted, St Augustine called even just wars "miseries" and "evils," and wrote that if anyone could think of them "without mental pain," that person "has lost human feeling." C.S. Lewis (who had himself been a soldier in the First World War) acknowledged in the quotation above that "war is a dreadful thing." There is also a long tradition of concern that killing, even in a just cause, holds great spiritual dangers. "Thus Basil the Great (Bishop of Caesarea in the fourth century A.D.): 'Killing in war was differentiated by our fathers from murder... nevertheless, perhaps it would be well that those whose hands are unclean abstain from communion for three years'."[22]

A Courageous Combination

Ideally, a Christian warrior should combine all of these ideas: a deep concern to avoid war wherever possible, and to fight only in just wars; a joyful, courageous approach to a war believed to be just; and great concern both for those killed (whatever their crimes, they are human beings) and for the warrior's own soul, since killing is inherently dangerous, at the very least, for a Christian.

Who May Decide if a War is Just?

We may begin by noting that the Church as the Church has no particular expertise or infallibility in declaring that a war is just or unjust, although Church leaders may have opinions. (Thus, the silence of the Church on any particular war means only that the Church leaves the evaluation of the criteria to others.)

Consider again the importance of the question. Starting a war is the most serious act a nation can undertake outside its borders. War loosens the ordinary constraints on those involved. Property is being destroyed, people are being killed, and those near a battle, if they have any warning, leave their property unguarded and run. Those surprised by a battle are unusually helpless. Soldiers and others have guns and other weapons, and cannot be supervised in any strict sense. In the midst of all this killing and destruction, rape, theft, and murder are often much easier to get away with than usual. The destruction and killing encourage an atmosphere of hatred and revenge. Even in a just war against their country, soldiers defending their homeland generally believe they are in the right. In an unjust war, such soldiers truly are in the right, and killing them is killing the innocent. To launch even a minor war is to set all these consequences in motion, which is why it is such a grave decision. All the heavier the responsibility if you are endeavouring to ensure that it is just.

Justice and Positions of Power

Justice is not easy to find in this world. As the Preacher reminds us (Ecclesiastes 1:15), “What is crooked cannot be made straight, and what is lacking cannot be numbered." We are all tempted to proclaim all our own actions just and fair, and even to persuade ourselves of this when deep down we know it is not true. This is especially the case for rulers, with their hands on the levers of power, and their ambition, often, to stay in power as long as possible. (Leaders are often both talented and ambitious, or they would not have achieved power.) As the Catholic thinker Lord Acton told us, "power tends to corrupt, and absolute power tends to corrupt absolutely." Psalm 146 (v. 3) says, in a slightly different context, "Put not your confidence in princes, in a son of man, in whom there is no help." This certainly does not mean that all rulers constantly lie and never act justly. Government has a legitimate though limited function in this world, and is entitled to respect as it fulfills that function. However, that respect may certainly be combined with a healthy doubt, especially in literate people with the ability to check up on the justifications their government offers for a war.

There was much criticism after the Second World War of educated Germans who simply accepted their government's statements about its intentions and actions. The criticism is legitimate, but the lesson is not, as is sometimes implied or stated, "Germans are not to be trusted," but that educated people generally are often prone to accept what their governments tell them, when in fact they should always be somewhat sceptical of them. Of course, a government proposing a good action that is well-supported by facts should have no fear of such scepticism and the resulting scrutiny, just as a good prosecutor does not fear the need to convince a sceptical jury of the prisoner's guilt.

Aquinas states that "the authority of the sovereign" is necessary for a just war. The fact that the sovereign's authority is necessary does not mean that the sovereign always rightly evaluates whether his proposed war meets the six criteria listed above. Yet when the rulers of a country propose a war, they will always try to persuade their citizens that it is just. If they are right, they will present facts to persuade citizens of their rightness. If they are wrong, and have an interest in fighting a war other than its justice, they will still make a case for war, this time shading or warping the truth (or misrepresenting it out of ignorance) in order to make the war appear just. Yet only the "sovereign," or the legitimate ruler, may rightly declare war. Where does that leave teachers, journalists, experts, bloggers, and ordinary citizens?

The Role of the Citizen

As noted above, the *Catechism* states that the "evaluation" of the criteria, in effect the decision to go to war, belongs to "the prudential judgment of those who have responsibility for the common good." Designated leaders have the greatest responsibility for the common good, and the authority to make such decisions. However, we all have some responsibility for the common good[23], especially under democratic systems of government. Those who are skilled at research and analysis have more responsibility than others. Those who can also write and speak persuasively have even more responsibility. While the responsibility of such citizens is not the same as that of those who actually declare war, it is a heavy responsibility nonetheless.

All aware citizens have an important role to play in deciding whether a proposed war is just or unjust, and in supporting or opposing it. Citizens and especially opinion leaders are responsible to inform themselves of the morality of war—ideally they will discover the just war theory criteria. They are then responsible, as far as they are able and have time and resources, to inform themselves of the facts that bear on the criteria. The more a person is listened to, as a teacher, leader, writer, or speaker, the heavier the responsibility to be informed and to judge rationally and carefully. In this context partisanship, the ugly habit of superficially questioning leaders from "my" party while easily entertaining the deepest doubts about leaders from "the other" party, is a grave fault. It distracts our fellow citizens from the truth, while urging them to be blinded by their emotions. Sadly, those who shout "partisanship" the loudest are often refusing to think clearly about "their" party's actions. Refusing to look at the possibility that the "other side," whether pro- or anti-war, is correct, or to look at sources cited by "the other side," is another grave fault. These are rarely the faults of just one side before or during a conflict, but we are never excused by saying, "the other side is appealing to raw emotion, twisting the facts, and making one-sided presentations, so we are free to do so as well."

The Burden of Proof

One more factor to bear in mind is that the burden of proof lies on those proposing a war, unless it is clearly, unquestionably defensive in nature. In the latter case, all who care about their country should be willing to help defend it in some way. If a war is not clearly defensive, then the decision to launch it is similar in intensity to the decision to sentence a man or woman to death, but on a far grander scale. It would be gravely and obviously wrong to sentence a man to death without (at the least) a case for his guilt that is beyond reasonable doubt. A declaration of war, even a planned "small" war, is equivalent to a sentence of death for dozens, or perhaps hundreds or even hundreds of thousands (since many wars grow far beyond the plans of those who start them). Many or most of the victims of war are innocent of any crime. Clearly the same standard, "beyond reasonable doubt," applies. If the anti-war writers and speakers cast serious doubt on the pro-war case, citizens should oppose the planned war, unless the pro-war speakers and writers can overcome that doubt with good evidence. Just as the "presumption of innocence" strengthens the jury's final judgment of guilt in a court case, so the belief that the burden of proof rests on the pro-war side in any non-defensive war can only lead to greater certainty that a decision to go to war is correct.

(Note: soldiers who join a nation's military should not simply be seeking adventure or a paid education, but should also be confident in the moral judgment of their leaders. If that is the case, they may safely listen to the judgment of their officers and leaders concerning the justice of a proposed war, although they should certainly listen to their consciences as well. It is generally assumed that officers have a greater responsibility to be informed than the enlisted, and the higher their rank and the greater their thinking ability, the less they are entitled simply to accept the judgment of their superiors. This leads to the uncomfortable result that when an intelligent, well-informed officer decides a proposed war is clearly unjust, he is obligated by his conscience not to support it.)

Another Source: International Law

In addition to the reasoning noted above, the Catholic Church considers nations to be bound by their obligations under international law. Generally, these obligations are based on commitments nations have made by signing various treaties. Concerning the *ius ad bellum*, the most important of these treaties at this point in history is the United Nations Charter, which each member state of the United Nations ratified when it joined. Nations that signed the UN Charter accepted many obligations, one of the most important of which is the obligation not to use force in international relations without the authorization of the UN Security Council, except, in emergency situations, in self-defense. While some Catholic writers downplay or ignore the importance of this commitment, it is actually quite straightforward, as anyone may see by looking up the Charter. Solemn commitments freely entered into are morally binding. The only moral way to escape this obligation would be to repudiate the UN Charter and leave the United Nations.

The Arms Race: When Too Much is Too Much

Catholic social teaching on war includes a warning against the belief that security rests on ever-increasing amounts of weaponry. As the *Catechism* notes, "This method of deterrence gives rise to strong moral reservations. The arms race does not ensure peace. Far from eliminating the causes of war, it risks aggravating them."[24] It would be easy to misinterpret this statement as a prohibition on spending for armaments, or a total contradiction of the idea that a peace-loving nation may have weapons and forces prepared for war. In fact, it is quite possible, under Catholic teaching, to believe that a nation is spending too little on war-fighting capabilities. On the other hand, the teaching warns that it is easy to spend too much. To be automatically "left-wing" and always against military spending, or "right-wing" and always in favor of it, are both false positions in terms of Catholic teaching. The level of military spending should be dictated by prudence, guided by faith. On the one hand, a naïve trust in the good intentions of other countries is not part of Catholic teaching, and a lack of military capability may invite aggression by neighboring governments seeking resources or territory. On the other hand, no risk can be entirely eliminated in this world. A massive build-up of "defensive" forces can lead rival nations to conclude, reasonably, that they are being targeted in some way, and may also lead the people of the heavily-armed nation to believe more easily that military force is the best or even only solution to their nation's perceived problems.

Terror and Terrorism

Terror is a tactic. A terrorist act may be defined as any act in which civilians are intentionally targeted in order, through wounding or killing them, to change some group or government's policy, or to produce some new state of affairs in the world. It is this purpose that defines an act as terrorist, for those who kill or wound for no particular reason, or to steal or for personal satisfaction of some other kind, are simply criminals. We tend to think of terrorist groups in this context (but the question is not at all so simple, see below). A "terrorist group" may be defined as a group that employs terrorist acts as its predominant mode of action, and a "terrorist" as someone who engages in such acts.

Catholic teaching unreservedly condemns all such acts, whoever commits them. They are examples of assaults, in a sense, on God himself through assaults on his image. To put it another way, they are examples of "doing evil that good may come." Those who excuse such actions, no matter who engages in them or what the cause, should be asked what standards they can possibly be upholding if they are willing to destroy innocent human beings in order to produce a political effect. If they have no moral standards for the moment, how can they hope to produce good results, and why should anyone believe they will suddenly apply moral standards in the future?

"Terrorism" is a misleading term, in that it suggests a parallel with such terms as communism or capitalism. Those names suggest something about the society the followers of the "ism" want to create, rather than the tactics they plan to use to establish it. However, even the most grotesque groups using terror as a tool, for example the Khmer Rouge, who slaughtered about a third of the people of Cambodia, have had an aim other than terror itself: a new society of some kind.

Good and Evil

In fact, there is a great deal more confusion about terror and terrorism in our media and daily speech. First, terrorist groups are often assumed to be examples of pure evil in this world. However, Catholic teaching (and a careful look at the world) reveals that while there is hideous evil in the world, no human being is completely devoid of either good or evil. As Aleksandr Solzhenitsyn put it so magnificently, "Gradually it was disclosed to me that the line separating good and evil passes not through states, nor between classes, nor between political parties either—but right through every human heart—and through all human hearts."[25] If Solzhenitsyn is right (and all Catholic teaching supports the thought), then drawing the good vs. evil line between groups is a quick route to confusion. And, as we have seen, what makes an act an act of terror is its purpose. It is just to condemn the act, but to deny or ignore the stated purpose is to condemn oneself to lesser understanding of our fellow humans. The stated grievances behind the act may be real ones, and movements that use terror at one point often later become respectable governments—so much are good and evil mixed in this world. We should be willing to consider the claimed reasons for terrorist acts, even as we (always) condemn the acts. We may learn that the targets of the terrorists have themselves done some evil, or are continuing to do so. Some Chechens have committed terrorist acts, for example, but Russian armed forces have committed atrocities as well against Chechen civilians. Condemning only terrorists, or assuming that they can have no genuine grievances, will cause us to misunderstand the world.

Acts of War

Second, many actions that are condemned as "terrorist" are actually attacks on soldiers, by groups that have in effect declared war on those soldiers and the state behind them. These acts do not fit the definition above. They are acts of war (and their war may be either just or unjust). If such acts are terrorist, then the out-of-uniform American patriots who shot at British soldiers from behind trees were terrorists. Someone may object that if a member of a terrorist group attacks soldiers, it is an act of terrorism because of who the attacker is: a terrorist. This is confusion. An act is good or bad, just or unjust, because of the act itself and the circumstances, not because of the label on the actor. Sound moral judgment is not a matter of dueling labels.

Terror as Part of Government Policy

Thirdly, soldiers and other members of formal governments also sometimes commit terrorist acts. The example of the Khmer Rouge was given above. That group began as an insurgency against an established government. However, it was after it took over Cambodia that it committed its most hideous acts of terror. Throughout history there are examples of organized armies that have caused harm to or killed civilians as a way of attempting to influence people not to collaborate with an insurgency or to surrender quickly. Many governments have consciously directed their armed forces to slaughter groups of civilians with a variety of weapons, including artillery and bombs dropped from aircraft or carried by missiles. Such actions are terrorist in their nature. The fact that they are committed by an entity called a "government" does not change that fact. In some cases, terror is clearly a part of the policy of the government, and the drive to commit terrorist acts flows from the top down. In other cases, individual officers or even soldiers may take matters into their own hands. Each such action is morally ugly and wrong, no matter who may have conceived or ordered it.

Finally, it should not be forgotten that some actions by governments are as evil as or even more evil than acts of terror in their total effects. For example, sanctions that prevent a government from obtaining vital supplies to protect the basic health of its people can lead to widespread preventable deaths of civilians. The same is true of acts that aim at military targets but kill disproportionate numbers of civilians. In both of these cases a government is effectively committing murder on a large scale, and sometimes for the same reasons as terrorist groups: to cause a group or government to change a policy, or to create a new political or military situation in the world. The numbers of civilians affected are sometimes far larger than the number of civilians killed in many terrorist attacks.

A War on Terrorism

In light of all this, the idea of a "war on terrorism" is a difficult one, with many possible confusions involved. First, we cannot ever totally prevent groups or governments from using terror in this world, any more than we can totally prevent individuals from murdering, or governments from starting unjust wars. On the other hand, if the term terrorism is taken to mean any ideology that supports the use of terror to achieve political or military aims, then this booklet is a part of a war on terrorism in that sense, as it attempts to persuade readers that the tactic of terror is morally wrong. However, an unusually large number of authors would need to be targeted in such a war (including some Catholic authors)[26]. If the term is taken to mean hunting down and killing any people who simply believe (without acting on it) in the use of terror, then this cannot be a just cause for a war. People should not be killed for their beliefs alone, however odious or dangerous.

However, the term "war on terrorism" may also be taken as short-hand for a physical war on members of certain groups that have used acts of terror, or perhaps on certain groups whose principle activities are centered around terrorist acts. Groups or governments that plan and implement terrorist attacks may certainly be held to account for such actions. It is almost certain that such actions would provide a just cause for a war—but that is only one part of what makes a war just, as pointed out above.

The Right Way to Fight a War

"War is hell," said the American general Sherman. We often see something like the following: "war is immoral, so once a war starts the best thing to do is to win quickly, whatever it takes."[27] This thought is quite contrary to Catholic teaching. As ugly as war is, the moral law applies to whether a war should be fought at all, as we have seen. It also applies within a war. The branch of just war theory dealing with right and wrong actions in a war is known as *ius in bello*, Latin for (roughly) "right in war."

Intrinsically Evil Means Such as Torture are Forbidden

First, although killing and destruction are allowed in a just war, they are not allowed in an unlimited way. More broadly, the Ten Commandments are not suspended. Rape and torture, for example, continue to be wrong.[28]

Perhaps rape is rarely defended as a conscious instrument of war. Torture, on the other hand, has had many defenders in recent years. Often, a "dilemma" is presented: a terrorist leader is captured, and is believed to have information (the location of bombs set to go off in the next twenty-four hours, for example) that will save the lives of innocents if it can be extracted from him. However, he refuses to talk. Since he has been trained to resist giving information, only severe measures seem likely to make him talk. For the sake of the lives of innocents that can be saved, it is argued, the terrorist leader must be tortured.[29]

Agonising as the fact of possible future deaths is in this situation, Catholic teaching does not accept this line of argument. Of course Catholic teaching condemns attacks on innocents, such as the bombings that the terrorist is believed to know about. These are despicable, evil acts. However, the fact that another person or group has done or is doing evil does not excuse me or my group doing evil. Perhaps this is easier to see on a small scale. If someone threatens to kill my brother if I do not hand over a sum of money, that does not justify me in killing his sister, even if I think doing so may prevent his killing my brother. Killing his sister would be a purely evil action, whatever I might hope it would lead to. The number of people involved does not substantially change the argument.

There are many reasons for this refusal to justify doing evil in the hope of preventing evil. Perhaps most importantly, the nation that authorises torture becomes evil to the extent that it does so. The same is true of the persons who perform it. Torture is an assault on the dignity of the human person, a dignity that rests on the fact that all human beings are created in the image of God, an image reinforced in the incarnation of Christ, who was willing to die to win us back and who now shares our humanity forever. A person may be punished, or force may be used to prevent him from doing an evil he is in the process of doing, precisely in order to protect the image of God which he is attacking. To put it another way, the government that authorises torture commits evil in the same kind of way as the group of terrorists, thus destroying at least part of the reason people should support it rather than the terrorists.

In addition, one action rarely sits alone in the way the imagined situation puts it. Instead, it is part of a series of actions. The government that is considering torturing the terrorist may have killed the terrorist's brother, or its soldiers may have raped his cousin. The justification, "we will do evil in the short term in order to prevent a greater evil" often justifies what turns out to be part of a string of evil actions that, in practice, may be endless.

There are even practical reasons for rejecting the idea of torture to gain information. Many of those selected for torture may have no useful information. In such a case, one is committing evil on the off chance that some other evil may be prevented, obviously a terrible bargain in moral terms. In other cases, the person being tortured is likely to be able to guard the most timely and important information while gradually giving out useless or false information, diverting the government's resources in directions where they will be wasted. A number of persons who have been charged with interrogating prisoners of war have claimed that the best way to gain accurate information is to treat the person humanely. Persons willing to die for their beliefs are most likely to hand out accurate information if they decide their beliefs are wrong.

It appears that there is an element of faith in this refusal to do evil (just as many good actions, and many refusals to do what is known to be wrong, are done by faith). It appears that we will lose if we do not do evil ourselves, but we should in fact believe that God will, in the end, reward our refusal to do what is wrong. A country or a civilization that chooses to do evil in order to save itself may in fact be hastening its own demise, whereas the refusal to make that choice may lead to a better fate, despite short-term calculations. (Conquering forces, like Hitler's army in the Soviet Union, have often through brutality against local people lost the chance to be seen as liberators, provoking resistance and savage vengeance when the tables were turned.) At any rate, there is a sense in which we do not control our destinies as people or as nations. They rest in God's hands—something not easy to explain or understand, but a belief that is often an element in the refusal of a person or nation to perform evil acts.

Non-Combatants May Not be Targeted

Second, although this may be controversial in the English-speaking world due to recent history, "for men to choose to kill the innocent as a means to their ends is always murder, and murder is one of the worst of human actions."[30] In the context of war, the innocent are those who are neither engaged in combat, nor engaged in supplying combatants with weapons or ammunition. Since the beginning of the twentieth century at least, wars have tended to involve the whole of society. Arguments can be made that everyone in a country has some connection to the "war effort." Despite this, the Catholic Church insists on the very old distinction between combatants and non-combatants, and insists that the deliberate targeting of non-combatants is murder.

This is one of many areas where just war theory may be uncomfortable. This prohibition of deliberate attacks on civilians leads to a clear condemnation, for example, of the attacks of September 11, 2001. But it also leads to a clear condemnation of many British and American bombing raids on German and Japanese cities during World War II.[31] Many such raids were openly designed to take the lives of large numbers of civilians, with little or no military justification, other than demoralising the surviving people into wanting to surrender. The most extreme of such raids were, of course, the two nuclear bombings of Hiroshima and Nagasaki. By this teaching, such raids were war crimes: murder on a vast scale. The response that they "hastened the end of the war" may be argued against in practical terms[32], but, more importantly, it is a morally ugly argument.

To see this, compare murder on a large scale to other evil acts that could have been chosen to hasten the end of the war: for example the rape of all German or Japanese women in captured territory, or the gruesome torture of or medical experiments on all prisoners of war. Would we have been justified in saying "the deliberate rape of all German women in cities we captured was acceptable because it hastened the end of the war"? What about "all Japanese prisoners of war were subjected to painful and crippling medical 'experiments,' which was acceptable because it hastened the end of the war"? Surely it is clear upon some reflection that to commit such acts knowingly is to become evil: not pure evil, as all human beings retain some fragment of good, but as evil as a multiple murderer or rapist is.

What about civilians living or working near military targets? Attacks on military targets are allowed even if some civilians may be killed accidentally during the attacks. In this case, the intention of the attacker is to destroy the military target, not to kill the civilians. (In a similar way, anyone may employ deadly force to defend her life against an attacker if necessary, because her primary intention is not to kill the attacker, but to save her life.) This is sometimes known as "double effect" reasoning: the desired effect is the destruction of the military target, and the secondary effect, which was not the aim of the action, is the death of a limited number of civilians.

An immediate qualification must be added: the accidental deaths of civilians must be in proportion to the military value of the target. This principle cannot be formulated in mathematical terms, but that does not mean it is meaningless. We might consider two extreme cases: in one, a group of five enemy soldiers is known to be regularly using a footbridge, beside which is a building outside which many children are often seen. A bomb that will destroy the bridge will likely kill many children in the building, which appears to be a school or orphanage. It is hard to imagine many people accepting this likely cost as "proportional." In a second case, the bridge in question is a railway bridge that carries dozens of trains, with thousands of soldiers, per week. If stopping the soldiers' transport is vital to the war, and there is no other sure way to stop the trains besides blowing up the bridge, most observers would likely conclude that this tragic accidental killing is, in fact, proportional. (There are also accidents of intelligence in war, where analysts believe a building or compound is military but it turns out to be civilian, etc.) In addition, proportionality applies over time: while the deaths of a certain number of civilians may be proportional in a given raid or attack, they may not be proportional in a long series of raids or attacks.

Insurgencies and Guerrilla Warfare

Guerrilla or insurgent warfare must also be considered in light of this prohibition of deliberate or disproportionate attacks on civilians. In such a conflict, the forces of one side are far weaker than the other in purely military terms. If they marched their troops into "the field" to attack conventional forces, they would simply be wiped out in hours. While the American insurgents of 1776 were democrats (in a limited sense by today's standards: they were not fighting for the rights of women, slaves, and non-property holders in many cases), many insurgents are not—yet they have the sympathy of many members of the population. This is often because the government is relying on foreign troops, or sometimes troops from a culturally different part of the country. The insurgents build on their popular support by dressing like civilians, blending into the population, and carrying out hit-and-run attacks against conventional forces. "Insurgents" or guerrilla forces generally do not try to hold territory for long: if attacked, they retreat. They ambush the conventional forces while on patrol, or in remote outposts, or they attack supply lines. Even if they behave harshly toward local people, that is sometimes seen by many local people as the only way to oust the "foreigners," or the "puppet" government.

Armies fighting insurgencies tend to take advantage of their conventional military superiority, greater firepower, and control of the air, but this leads to a dilemma. The insurgents fight from houses and local buildings. When a bomb is dropped on a building that a handful of insurgents are using, temporarily, as cover, the insurgents may be killed—along with the families that lived in the building. Or the bomb will, often enough, miss and hit the house next door. Because the insurgents share language, culture, and religion with the people around them, there is natural sympathy for them, and the foreign troops or the unpopular, foreign-supported government, and not the insurgents, are blamed for such deaths (which are, of course, not the direct responsibility of the insurgents). The insurgents have lost men, but have gained sympathy and new recruits, and local people are more willing to help at least by hiding them. Support for the government, which seems to care only for the safety of its troops, not of the civilians who died, has dropped.

In many cases, it is extremely difficult to kill any insurgents/guerrillas in such a setting without killing nearly as many or perhaps many more civilians. Thus, battle against insurgents can be counter-productive: as in the myth of Hercules and the Hydra, where from the stump of each head he cut off sprang two new heads.

Politically, each battle is a loss. Yet not fighting apparently means losing. At times it seems the only way to defeat such insurgents is to kill civilians in near-genocidal numbers, which is clearly wrong (and even this may not be enough to win against a widely-supported insurgency). It seems that on the one hand if government forces follow just war theory rules of warfare, they will continually lose small numbers of troops due to the restraint they are practicing. This is not a happy situation for the government(s) and army fighting the insurgents.

Before going to war, a government must consider whether this is the kind of warfare it will likely be involved in. A long, long series of decisions to destroy houses in which civilians are likely to be living may mean the destruction committed during the war will be out of proportion to ends for which it is being fought, rendering it an unjust war. Also, the fact that the civilians are continually dying may cause the government to lose credibility with the local people, defeating its ability to win the war. Any time a government sends its troops into another country without clearly announced time limits, it risks an insurgency, especially if those troops have a culture, religion, language, and customs that differ sharply from those of local people. This suggests that there is a sharp limit to how much good one country can do for another, especially through sending troops to take it over. This factor must be carefully weighed by a country considering whether it can wage a just war in another country. It is likely that the longer its troops stay in that other country, the more they will provoke a generalised insurgency by their presence. Unless the invading country can quickly establish a stable new government after overthrowing the old, and then quickly minimize its presence, or, better, remove its troops, it may be that the "reasonable chance of success" becomes a very small chance. If that is the case, the war should not be started. This makes it all the more important, then, to have a clear, detailed, and realistic vision of success before starting a war.[33]

The Wounded, Those Who Surrender, Prisoners

It was pointed out above that non-combatants must not be targeted. Seriously wounded soldiers are generally out of combat, and as the Catechism states, "must be respected and treated humanely"[34]. The same is true of soldiers attempting to surrender, and prisoners. There are times when this imposes serious costs on the army that can take prisoners. It may be dangerous to transport prisoners out of the war zone (rather than killing them), or expensive to feed them even a minimal diet. However, facing such risks or costs is a moral duty imposed on all armed forces.

War: Other Issues

The Crusades

The Crusades are often thrown at Catholics as examples of unjust wars in the past endorsed or launched by the Church. For a more in-depth look at the Crusades than this booklet can provide, the CTS "concise history" booklet *The Crusades* provides a great deal of light. Here, it may be said that each generation must be judged in light of the possibilities existing when it lived. Next, the vast majority of the Crusades appear to have been defensive in several senses: first, they were attempts to re-take for Christendom lands that had been forcefully seized from Christian kingdoms (or the Christian Byzantine Empire) by Islamic invaders. True, that Islamic invasion was centuries earlier in some instances, but it is not as if Christian forces suddenly invaded Islamic areas that had never been Christian. (In addition, it seems thoroughly hypocritical to complain about the Crusades without complaining about the earlier and later Islamic invasions as well.) Second, in many cases there were complaints about Christian inhabitants or pilgrims being mistreated, either by the authorities or by bandits who were ignored by the Islamic authorities. Given that Islamic rule of all these areas began with a conquest, the responsibility to ensure the safety of inhabitants, or of pilgrims on long-standing routes to holy places, was a serious one. In light of these facts, it is often arguable at least that a just cause existed at the beginning of a crusade. The right intention to establish a peaceful rule in the area is easy enough to grant, and given that peasants and city-dwellers alike were not used to having much voice in how they were governed, the Crusaders did not think about democracy, and did not need to be as concerned as today about the likelihood of insurgencies against their planned rule. The sovereign authority criterion was clearly met in most cases (although divided authority among the different groups of soldiers presented a huge problem in many cases, see the booklet mentioned above).

The last three criteria, proportionality of ends, last resort, and reasonable chance of success, were more difficult to estimate at that time. It was more difficult to estimate the possible or likely costs of a war, or the damage likely to result (proportionality of ends, reasonable chance of success). There were fewer people who could speak the language of the other side, with less knowledge of the rest of the world for all sides, and communications were far slower, making it more difficult to explore other avenues besides war (last resort).

In terms of justice in going to war, we should also remember that according to Catholic teaching, popes, like other Catholics, are capable of both sin and errors of judgment. A decision that war was necessary to reverse Islamic conquests was not in the realm of faith and morals where, we believe, popes are preserved from error in their formal pronouncements as heirs to the promise of our Lord to St Peter. (On a related note, the popes had political as well as religious responsibilities at this time, as temporal rulers of much of what is now northern Italy.)

There is no doubt that many serious sins, many grave injustices, were committed by Crusaders during the fighting. While the picture of boorish, horrible Crusaders fighting cultured, gallant Muslims is a rather silly one, there is no point in denying the evil that was done at times by Crusaders (and by Muslim warriors, for that matter). But such evil was not the intention of the popes and preachers who called for the Crusades. They did not call for cities to be sacked and women to be raped: on the contrary, they called for the innocent to be protected. European Christians were and are capable of acting barbarically, as well as of responding to calls based on high ideals. Historians now note that after the Crusaders were driven out of the Middle East, the Islamic world basically forgot them: in the long term view, they were brief incursions that failed. Only later, when almost the entire Muslim world was under European rule, did Muslim writers begin to write extensively about the Crusades and compare them to their then-current troubles (a trend that continues). One reason earlier Muslims forgot them is that Muslim conquests of non-Muslim lands continued for long centuries after the Crusades. The Moghuls conquered Hindu northern India, and Islam continued to expand in Africa, sometimes by conquest. Under the Ottoman Turks, the entire Greek Orthodox world became part of the Turkish empire, as well as vast swathes of Christian Slavic lands, areas far wider than any the Crusades in the Middle East ever conquered. In many cases, such as Anatolia, or present-day Turkey, these Islamic conquests were never reversed. The history of Islamic-Christian relations is a complex one, and a picture of demonic Crusaders versus peace-loving Muslims is simply an unhelpful caricature. The Crusades were far from perfect in their implementation, and there was guilt on the part of those who committed war crimes, but the intent of those who called for the Crusades was not the slaughter and oppression of Muslim populations.

Spiritual Warfare

Every Christian is meant to be engaged in spiritual warfare. As members of the body of Christ, and of that part of it here on earth that is "the Church militant," all Catholics, and all Christians, are meant to be soldiers of Christ. Here, the rules are quite different from those of physical warfare. We are seeking Christ's Kingdom, with the weapons of the Kingdom. Our enemies are not the human beings who oppose the Church and the gospel—those we must love and pray for—but "the spiritual hosts of wickedness in the heavenly places." (Ephesians 6:12) The sovereign authority is God's, the right intention and the just cause the establishment of God's kingdom. There is no calculation of costs, no proportionality, no restraint, no thought of any response but (spiritual) war. Here at last we are dealing with the enemy some confusedly think they find in earthly foes: evil unmixed with any moral good.

A reliance on grace, a growth in our own virtues (which are gifts and are dependent on grace, but made ours in our practice of them), prayer for ourselves, those around us, the whole Church, and the world, and actions that embody love for those around us, are the daily prescribed "war" activities of every Christian. If we are not engaged in them daily, we can hardly be described as Christians or Catholics in any full sense of the words. Those names do not describe people with "tickets to heaven," but people who, as part of a spiritual army, are working with others to help fight for and build the kingdom of heaven. St Francis de Sales' *Introduction to the Devout Life* or St Jose-Maria Escriva's *The Way* provide classic guidance and encouragement in the struggle, and of course there are many others. We might say that the Eucharist provides our field rations, and regular confession helps keep us spiritually fit. "Spiritual reading:" the Bible, good explanations of it, and works by and about the saints, for example, reminds us of our orders from headquarters, of our strategy and tactics and war aims. St Francis de Sales, St Jose-Maria, and others point out the importance of spiritual direction in our lives. This is an amazing resource of the Catholic Church, although it must be sought: free guidance for the spiritual struggle each of us should be waging. Ask your parish priest where you can find it.

Deterrence and Preemption

The idea of deterrence is that a nation well-prepared to defend itself, or to punish an attack against itself, is therefore less likely (unless it is itself acting aggressively) to be attacked. Common sense tells us there is a great deal of truth in the idea. Many Biblical stories reinforce it. However, as noted in the section on the arms race, one danger of being very well-armed is a tendency to believe that military action is the solution to any problem. This is not an unavoidable danger, but is nevertheless real—in the same way that beautiful people may think their beauty is the solution to problems, the strong look to their strength, the rich to their money, and so forth. There is nothing inherently wrong with beauty, strength, or money, but those well-endowed with any of them need to learn humility if they wish to act virtuously, as we are all called to act. The same goes for military strength, and for a nation to purposely increase its military strength beyond any real need for it is at least as morally dangerous as it is for a person to put excessive efforts into a search for beauty, physical strength, or money.

While deterrence in general is a good thing for a peaceful nation, deterring attacks by having real plans to commit atrocities such as widespread attacks on civilians is wrong. Even the stratagem of convincing the "enemy" of intentions to commit such atrocities if attacked is dangerous, as the citizens and military leaders of the presumably virtuous country that is merely faking the plans for preemptive atrocities are likely to be encouraged to commit to them as real plans instead. It is unlikely that nations capable of such atrocities, such as nuclear powers, have no other means to respond to a possible attack.

Preemption, the idea of preventing a planned attack through attacking the presumed aggressor, is perhaps an even more complex issue. Generally, it is nearly impossible to be sure what an opponent is thinking or planning. There are, however, acts that are by tradition considered acts of war, such as an armed war fleet of Country A sailing into Country B's territorial waters without permission. In such a case, Country B clearly has a right to use force: but against the aggressive fleet, not against any forces of Country A whatsoever. As legal expert Christopher Greenwood notes, a preemptive response to a planned attack is sometimes legally acceptable, but only if the threat is "imminent." Greenwood approvingly quotes a letter of U.S. Secretary of State Daniel Webster to the British government in 1837, which argued that such a right exists only if there is "a necessity of self-defense, instant, overwhelming, leaving no choice of means and no moment for deliberation."[35] Where this kind of imminent danger is not present, there is no justification for an attack. Even in terms of logic, "preventive war" is a recipe for endless aggression by all sides, as each side will be encouraged to attack its "enemies" to "prevent" attacks by them. Where it has been tried the results have generally been disastrous (even if there is no doubt that in some cases the party attacked was truly planning aggression).

Pacifism

The Church teaches that the use of force is in fact sometimes justified. In addition, governments have "a right and duty" to force citizens to contribute to "the national defense".[36] Note first that this is not a blanket endorsement of military conscription, as it is limited to cases of national defense, rather than a general duty to serve in the armed forces. (Common sense tells us that the armed forces of the world act offensively as often as defensively: two parties in a war can scarcely both be defending themselves except in rare cases of complete misunderstanding.) Second, governments should give those whose consciences forbid them to fight alternate ways to serve in a time of defensive war.[37] Thus, while the Church does not teach pacifism, it teaches the duty of governments to make allowances for those whose consciences tell them never to use force.

However, one Catholic philosopher points out a danger in the idea of pacifism. G.E.M. Anscombe writes that the idea of pacifism encourages a "hypocrisy of the ideal standard." According to her, ordinary people often point to pacifism as an ideal they admire, but cannot follow, and therefore they feel excused in abandoning moral standards in war. War is evil, we must fight this war, and therefore we must do evil, they say: as much as is needed to win. Anscombe compares this to the false reasoning of a person committing fraud who says he admires "absolute honesty," but absolute honesty involves no private property, which is impossible, so he continues with his fraud. Anscombe, using the distinctions of Aristotle and Aquinas, says war is always evil in the sense that it involves the destruction of property and human life, but that those who fight rightly to protect human life are not doing moral evil.[38]

The Pope's 'Questions'

Shortly after the Iraq War began in 2003, then-cardinal Joseph Ratzinger, now Pope Benedict XVI, was asked whether Pope John Paul II believed the war met just war criteria.[39] Cardinal Ratzinger replied quite firmly that the pope believed the war did not meet the criteria. Cardinal Ratzinger was careful to point out that Pope John Paul II "did not impose this position as doctrine of the Church but as the appeal of a conscience enlightened by faith." He went on to say that "the Holy Father's judgment is also convincing from the rational point of view: There were not sufficient reasons to unleash a war against Iraq."

Some of the results of that war—estimates of hundreds of thousands of Iraqis dead, with millions of Iraqis fleeing their homes, with untold thousands wounded, robbed, or otherwise harmed in the chaos and fighting during and after the invasion—make the concern of Pope John Paul II and of the future Pope Benedict easily understandable. The grim situation of the remaining Christians in Iraq since that time reinforces the point.

Cardinal Ratzinger then posed a question: "given the new weapons that make possible destructions that go beyond the combatant groups, today we should be asking ourselves if it is still licit to admit the very existence of a 'just war.'" As we saw, the *Catechism* (the writing of which Cardinal Ratzinger helped supervise) insists on the possibility of a war that is just to fight, but also insists on "strict conditions" that must be "rigorously applied." Yet the then-cardinal's final question focuses not on the justice of going to war, but on the ways of fighting a war, on "new weapons" that so often leave non-combatants dead in large numbers. As a theologian of wisdom and intelligence who carefully follows current affairs, perhaps he was concerned by the tremendous "collateral damage" the new weapons are constantly causing when used in war, no matter how much "precision" they are often claimed to have.

At the very least, these questions from the future Pope Benedict XVI should leave Catholics concerned about the "rigour" with which just war criteria are applied, before, during, or even after a war, and sceptical of quick and easy claims that a given war meets them. In addition, we should probably be far more concerned than we often are about the deaths and maimings and woundings of civilians that so commonly accompany attacks on military targets. Just war theory insists that if these are intentional and not proportional, the killings involved are a form of murder. This must be taken far more seriously than it often is in our time.

Notes

[1] "The Challenge of Peace," paragraph 23, accessed 11 August 2010 at www.usccb.org.

[2] "Challenge," summary.

[3] "Challenge," paragraph 68.

[4] "Challenge," paragraph 111 to 114.

[5] Kenneth D. Whitehead, *One, Holy, Catholic, and Apostolic: The Early Church Was the Catholic Church* (San Francisco: Ignatius Press, 2000), 62-63.

[6] For a detailed look at Catholic views on religious and other freedoms, see the CTS booklet *Democracy & Tyranny: The Catholic Understanding of the State and Politics.*

[7] Thomas Aquinas, *Summa Theologica*, II-II, 40. (Note: the entire Summa may be found on-line at "New Advent:" www.newadvent.org (accessed 6 December 2007)). The verse quoted is Luke 3:14.

[8] Aquinas, *Summa*, II-II, 40.

[9] Pope Benedict XVI, the speech at the University of Regensburg, accessed 9 August 2010 at www.catholicculture.org.

[10] Aristotle, *The Nichomachean Ethics* (London: Penguin Books, 1976), 271.

[11] Marcus Tullius Cicero, *Commonwealth*, Introduction to the Third Book, in The Online Library of Liberty, accessed 18 November 2008 at oll.libertyfund.org. See also Cicero, De Officiis, Book I, xi, 34, accessed 18 November 2008 at www.stoics.com.

[12] Augustine, *The City of God*, Book 19, Chapter 15, Christian Classics Ethereal Library, accessed 11 August 2010 at www.ccel.org.

[13] *City of God*, Book 19, Chapters 5 and 7, accessed 4 December 2007 at www.ccel.org

[14] *Summa*, II-II, 40.

[15] This point was made by James Turner Johnson in "Just War as it Was and Is," *First Things*, no. 149 (January 2005): 17.

[16] *The Catholic Catechism*, paragraph 2309.

[17] For a detailed discussion of this point, see Craig M. White, *Iraq: the Moral Reckoning* (Maryland: Lexington Books, Inc., 2010) 235-7.

[18] See *Iraq*, 231-36.

[19] George Weigel, *Letters to a Young Catholic* (New York: Basic Books, 2004) 86-87 (Note: the application of the idea "stuff counts" to just war theory is the author's, not Weigel's).

[20] Hilaire Belloc, *The Path to Rome* (San Francisco: Ignatius Press, 2003), 130.

[21] C.S. Lewis, Mere Christianity (San Francisco: HarperCollins Publishers, Inc., 2001), 119.

[22] Michael Walzer, "Political Action: The Problem of Dirty Hands," in *War and Moral Responsibility* (Princeton: Princeton University Press, 1974), 69. See also James Turner Johnson, *The War to Oust Saddam Hussein: Just War and the New Face of Conflict* (Maryland: Rowman and Littlefield, 2005), 73-74. Johnson notes, "For a significant period in the Middle Ages in Western Europe, warriors after battle were required by church law to do penance before being readmitted to the sacraments—not because they might have killed other people…but because they might have done so out of wrong intention, including the desire to dominate others or a particular hatred toward another."

[23] *Gaudium et Spes*, para 74. See Iraq, 243, for a fuller discussion.

[24] *Catechism*, paragraph 2315.

[25] Aleksandr Solzhenitsyn, *The Gulag Archipelago* (New York: Harper and Row, Publishers, 1985), 312.

[26] See, for example, Michael Scheuer, *Marching Toward Hell: America and Islam after Iraq* (New York: Free Press, 2008), 76. "Perhaps more pertinent words for Americans, though harsher sounding, are those of the Civil War era's General Philip H. Sheridan. 'The main thing in true

strategy is simply this,' Sheridan wrote in his memoirs. 'First deal as hard blows at the enemy's soldiers as possible, and then cause so much suffering to the inhabitants of a country that they will long for peace and press their government to make it. Nothing should be left to the people but eyes to lament the war.'" Scheuer likewise is fond of quoting from Machiavelli, and openly disparages just war theory. It is a serious thing for a Catholic to endorse an amoral philosopher and to throw out twenty centuries of consistent Church teaching that Christian morality is to be applied in all areas of life. It also leads to a bizarre piece of circular logic: what is the moral value of fighting for the United States of America if the United States of America is amoral about its wars? Despite this crucial failing, Scheuer provides many useful insights and analyses.

[27] Scheuer's approving quotation of General Sheridan is just one example of many that could be given, from many authors.

[28] *Catechism*, paragraph 2312.

[29] See, for example, Walzer, "Dirty Hands," 68-69.

[30] G.E.M. Anscombe, "Mr. Truman's Degree", accessed 12 August 2010 at www.anthonyflood.com.

[31] *Catechism*, paragraph 2314.

[32] Anscombe, "Mr. Truman's Degree."

[33] The author is not an expert on guerrilla warfare or insurgencies. However, the following list, from an expert, would be useful for someone pursuing the subject: Mao Tse-Tung, *On Guerrilla Warfare* (Illinois, University of Illinois Press, 2000); David Galula, *Counterinsurgency Warfare: Theory and Practice* (Santa Barbara, California: Praeger, 2006); Sam C. Sarkesian, *Revolutionary Guerrilla Warfare: Theories, Doctrines, and Contexts* (Piscataway, New Jersey: Transaction Publishers, 2010); and John Mackinlay, *The Insurgent Archipelago*, (New York: Columbia University Press, 2009).

[34] *Catechism*, paragraph 2313.

[35] Christopher Greenwood, International Law and the Pre-emptive Use of Force: Afghanistan, Al-Qaida, and Iraq, 4 San Diego Int'l L.J. no 7, 13.

[36] *Catechism*, paragraph 2310.

[37] *Catechism*, paragraph 2311.

[38] Anscombe, "Mr. Truman's Degree."

[39] Cardinal Ratzinger was quoted in an interview with *Zenit* published 2 May 2003, accessed 29 July 2010 at www.ratzingerfanclub.com.

Disclaimer

The views expressed herein are either clearly a part of Catholic teaching on war and peace, or are intended by the author to be so, or, finally, are the author's own, more tentative views of the application of that teaching. Although the author worked for the United States Department of State at the time of publication, none of the views expressed herein are those of the Department of State, which does not endorse this book.